Solace

Elouise Miller
Hollenbaugh

WESTBOW
P R E S S®
A DIVISION OF THOMAS NELSON
& ZONDERVAN

WestBow Press books may be ordered through booksellers or by contacting:

WestBow Press
A Division of Thomas Nelson & Zondervan
1663 Liberty Drive
Bloomington, IN 47403
www.westbowpress.com
844-714-3454

Because of the dynamic nature of the Internet, any web addresses or links contained in this book may have changed since publication and may no longer be valid. The views expressed in this work are solely those of the author and do not necessarily reflect the views of the publisher, and the publisher hereby disclaims any responsibility for them.

Any people depicted in stock imagery provided by Getty Images are models, and such images are being used for illustrative purposes only. Certain stock imagery © Getty Images.

Scripture quotations marked (NIV) are taken from the Holy Bible, New International Version®, NIV®. Copyright © 1973, 1978, 1984, 2011 by Biblica, Inc.™ Used by permission of Zondervan. All rights reserved worldwide. www.zondervan.comThe "NIV" and "New International Version" are trademarks registered in the United States Patent and Trademark Office by Biblica, Inc.™

ISBN: 978-1-6642-0788-2 (sc)
ISBN: 978-1-6642-0787-5 (hc)
ISBN: 978-1-6642-0934-3 (e)

Library of Congress Control Number: 2020920167

Print information available on the last page.

WestBow Press rev. date: 11/06/2020

The following poems were inspired by essays written by my friend, John Vander Velden (Author of Misty Creek), who graciously gave me permission to include these in my book.

Christmas
Poems

That Special Day

Christmas shopping is almost done.
Have I forgotten anyone?
I've trimmed the tree with sparkling lights
Each one adds to the festive sights.
Christmas songs fill the room with cheer.
That special day is almost here.
Holiday food soon to prepare
For family and friends all to share.
The crèche is in its usual place
On the mantle for all to embrace.
Baby Jesus lying on the hay;
The wise men bowing their heads to pray;
The sheep and lambs are resting near by;
The guiding star shines up in the sky.
All seems to be done, just one more thing:
Christmas cheer to all, I gladly bring.
May the story of His Holy birth
Help you to celebrate His great worth.

Christmas Cheer

Twas the night before Christmas and we wondered this year
If there would be any hope, would there be any cheer?
Stuck in a cardboard box was a little pine tree
No taller than Grandpa's arthritic knee.
On the floor around the tree everything was bare,
No packages piled up like used to be there.
We held hands and sang carols and songs of the season,
Then came thoughts of Christmas and its real reason.
As we looked at each other our faces lit up with a smile
Thinking of that very first Christmas for a while.
Then we read the story from the Bible of that special day
When Jesus was born in Bethlehem in a stable far, far away.
The star shining in the heavens was my favorite part.
It reminded me of finding Jesus and His presence in our heart.
No longer without hope, no longer without joy
We worshipped that Child, that special little Boy
And we discovered that presents didn't make Christmas cheer
It was knowing about Jesus and having Him near.

The True Son of God

There was a Baby born the end of a long day
In a lowly stable, lain in a manger of hay.
His mother was Mary, a special chosen maid.
His father was Joseph, a carpenter by trade.
The Child was the true Son of God up above
Who sent Him to earth to teach us His love.
We celebrate His birth in many ways
And raise our hearts in grateful praise.

What Do I Think of Christmas?

What do I think of Christmas?
How does it make me feel?
I think of Christmas as happiness
And a joy that is so real.
I think of it as presents
And a child's delightful squeal.
I think of it as going to church
And hearing the church bells peal.
I think of it as visits to family
Living so far away.
I think of it as Baby Jesus
Lying in a manger of hay.
I think of it as the shepherds
In their fields afar
Who heard the Angels message
To follow that heavenly star.
I think of it as the gifts
The wise men humbly brought
To give to the Child
Whom they relentlessly sought
I think of the lowly stable
Full of warmth and joy and love.
And, how the heavenly angels
Watched Him from above.
I think of it as a time
When we all should share
The gift of God's wonderful love
To people everywhere,
I think of it as hearing

The most melodious song
Sung by a church choir
With voices so loud and strong.
Announcing to all the world
That Christ the Savior is born
And through His gracious love
We are all reborn.

The Christ Child

A lowly stable manger filled with hay
Used for the newborn's bed at end of day.
Mary, His mother, watching her precious child
Laid her head close to His and knowingly smiled.
The prophesied Miracle Child was He
Born of a virgin, as God did decree.
Name Him Jesus, the angel had declared.
He is the Child who has been prepared
To bring people to know right from wrong.
The Child for whom so many do long.
Joseph, His earthly father, watched close by
Watching a bright star shining in the sky.
It appeared hovering overhead that night.
Shining brightly with a special heavenly light.
It seemed to say, "Someone special lies here".
'Tis the Christ Child we shall worship and revere.

Merry Christmas to All

Holidays are near
World's full of cheer
Tree time lighting
Weather is biting
Presents are sought
The right ones bought
Placed under the tree
For you and me
The Crèche displayed
Carols are played
A ride in the sleigh
In the snow to play
We hear the drum
The day has come
To celebrate the birth
Of Christ on Earth
Many wishes to you
And a Blessed Christmas, too.

The Prophesied Son

A Merry Christmas to everyone!
Come; Let's honor the Holy Son.
His mother, Mary, so brave and bold
Followed the message the Angel told.
A little child within her grew
Even though no man she knew.
Joseph took her as his wife
Knowing there would be scorn and strife.
They had to travel a very long way
For taxing laws they must obey.
With Mary close by his side
Upon a donkey she did ride.
Thus to Bethlehem they went
Fulfilling the prophesied event.
Joseph wondered what to do
Since rooms to rent were very few.
The carpenter did his very best
To find a place for his wife to rest.
There was a stable with empty space
Next to the animals; the only place.
The Baby was born that cold dark night.
And, the angels marveled at the sight
Of the Baby lying by the sheep
Wrapped in swaddling clothes to sleep.
A star shone upon the spot
Where God's miracle was brought

Fulfilling the prophecy of old
That in the Bible had been foretold.
He became the King of Kings
And all the world His virtue sings.
Amen! Hallelujah! Amen!

The Manger Child

A little child in a manger lay.
Born in a stable one cold day.
His mother, Mary smiled at Him
Even though the light was dim.
She saw His glowing baby face
And held Him in a warm embrace.
The Angel's message to Mary came true.
This was the true Son of God, she knew.
Her husband Joseph knelt and prayed
And, on God's Son his hand he laid.
He knew the job that must be done
As His earthly father, his work begun.
A carpenter by trade was he
With Baby Jesus at his knee.
He taught Him all the things he must
And in God's hands he put His trust.
The child grew in wisdom and grace.
The Holy Temple was His favorite place.
People wondered at this wondrous child
Whose character was so sweet and mild.
This little child whom from a manger came
Bears the sweetest Holy name.
JESUS the Son of God, lest we forget,
Was sent to earth to pay our debt
We celebrate His birth these days
In various places, in many ways.
My wish this Christmas---My main goal
Is to know that you have asked Jesus
To save your soul.

The Angel's Message

Mary was chosen to carry God's child.
For God had looked upon her and smiled
He sent an Angel with a message for her
From which she would not deter.
After hearing the message the Angel told
To obey she knew she must be bold.
And even though she was yet unwed
And had never slept in any man's bed
She accepted God's command to her
Even if ridicule she might incur.
Joseph, to whom she was betrothed
Concerned about what this would bode
Was visited by an Angel who said
Joseph, you have nothing to dread,
For this Child is from God above.
It is characteristic of His Holy Love.
So take this woman as your wife
And continue your holy Christian life.
The Child will grow to be good and kind
For He has been sent to save mankind
From sin that dwells within their heart
And as it is written, He will depart
And live in Heaven with His Father above
But leave with us His Precious love.

Mary's Child

An Angel came to Mary one night
Enshrouded by a heavenly light.
She was frightened by the sudden form
That came to her to inform
That she had been the chosen one
To bare a child God's only son.
How could she, a lowly maiden,
Have this longed for prophecy laden.
As she listened to the Angel's voice
Her heart jumped and did rejoice.
She knew that many people sought
For the news that this Angel brought.
But, as a lowly unmarried girl
Would others upon her, slander hurl?
But being a woman strong and brave
As God's follower she would behave.
So Joseph took here as his wife
And thus began their married life.
And while in the womb the baby lay
Mary visited her cousin, Elizabeth one day
Who was also full of humble pride
Since she too had a child inside.
Elisabeth's baby jumped within the womb
When the unborn Son of God entered the room.
Even though not yet full term
He knew this child he could affirm.
While her child was yet unborn
Mary and Joseph left early one morn
To pay their taxes that were due.

And as to Bethlehem they drew
There was no place for them to rest.
A stable they found to be the best.
The Baby came that very night
Surrounded by a heavenly light.
He had come! The Son of God!
The news was spread all abroad.
People honor and praise His Birth
For He is the Savior of our Earth.

They Called Him Jesus

The truth was told
By profits of old
Of a babe to be born
Whom some would scorn.
They called Him Jesus!

Mary watched o'er the little one
As Joseph admired his first born son.
This Child so beautiful and small
Born in a humble lowly stall.
They called Him Jesus!

Wise men found the shed
Where His manger bed
Was lined with hay
Where the animals lay
They called Him Jesus!

A star shone o'er the place
Where His holy face
Would shine with the peace
That could make wars cease.
They called Him Jesus!

Angels sang of the Holy One
God's true, precious Son
A very special Holy event
That ended with His holy ascent.
They called Him Jesus!

We celebrate His birth
With joy and mirth
Sharing what we've heard
From His Holy Word.
We call Him Jesus!

The Babe

There was a Babe born long ago
Whom everyone should love and know.
He was the Son of God above
Who sent Him here to share His love.
He gave His life on Calvary's tree
To save all sinners like you and me.
He left with us the Holy Spirit
To guide us on our way
So we would have eternal life
In Heaven with Him some day.

That Little Boy

Christmas is a time
For real peace and joy,
When we all celebrate
That precious little Boy,
Who was miraculously born
of the Virgin Mary.
The Child God's Angel predicted
she would carry.
He was born in a stable
so very, very small,
The animals stood over Him
Watching from their stalls.
The Angels sang a
heavenly chorus
That announced this
Child's birth for us.
A special star was
extra bright that night,
Leading shepherds to Him
with its guiding light.
Three wise men came to see Him
as the story is told.
Bringing precious gifts of
Frankincense, Myrrh and Gold.
This Child, the Son of God,
is the savior of us all.
And to someday live in Heaven,
upon His name we must call.

The Christmas Story

An angel came to Mary
As she lay sleeping in her bed.
You will bear the Son of God
And name Him Jesus, is what he said.

She became the wife of Joseph
A man who was very good.
He was a carpenter
Who made things out of wood.

The law said they must pay taxes
In the town where their family was from.
So they had to travel
To the town of Bethlehem.

The trip along the dusty road
Was long and rather dreary
But Joseph and his pregnant wife
Tried to stay calm and cheery.

When they finally arrived
In the town of Bethlehem
They found the crowded Inn
Had no room for them.

But the kind innkeeper agreed
That he would be able
To put them both up
In a lowly stable.

There Mary settled in
With Joseph standing nearby
And then they noticed a star
Sparkling brightly in the sky.

So Mary had the Baby
That very chilly night
While that star was shining
Overhead so very bright.

She laid the Baby in a manger
Wrapped in swaddling clothes.
She named the Baby Jesus
The name that God had chose.

The Little Donkey

I'm just a little donkey
that loves to sing and dance.
I'd like to do great things
if I'd only get a chance.
Papa plows the garden
with the farmer every day,
That's the way he helps
in his own special way.
Mama pulls the cart
that takes the buckets to the well,
And pulls the cart to market
with lots of stuff to sell.
Big brother turns the wheel
that grinds seed into meal.
He goes around in circles
turning a wooden wheel.
Sister pulls wheat on mats
from the field when it is ready
She pulls it to the barn
very slow and steady.
But I'm too small to be of help,
is what they always say.
They just put me in the barn
to keep me out of the way.
They say I'm much too little
and my ears are kinda long.
So I sit here in this stable
singing my sad, sad song
And then one night I saw a star

looking down on me
It seemed to say
"follow me and a wondrous thing you'll see.
So I walked out next morning
to see what it could be.
But all I found out there
were people walking on the road.
Heading for Bethlehem
with their meager load.
One of them, I noticed,
was very large with child.
I walked right up to her
as she seemed
so meek and mild.
Her husband smiled
then laid down his little sack
And lifted her and placed her
on my humble back.
Do you think possibly
you could carry her a while?
I nodded my head
which jiggled my long ears.
The young woman smiled
knowing she had no fears.
We traveled down a road
that led to Bethlehem
The Inns were all too full
and had no room for them.
So we had to stay
in a shed with just one gable.
It was just like where I live,
in a little stable.
A star was shining brightly

in the sky that night.
And seemed to give the manger
a special glowing light.
That very night was special
as the little Baby came
For I heard them say that
Jesus was His name.

Christmas Is For Children

Christmas is for children on that we all agree.
Their faces are all filled with such wonder and such glee,
Their anticipation flows with each and every day
Making sure behavior is always kept at bay.
Decorating cookies and yummy Christmas treats;
Those cookies that Santa always comes and eats.
Singing Christmas carols to friends all over town
Then to bed and lying their little sleepy heads down.
Anxious for the presents Santa leaves under the tree
While their parent are relaxing with a hot cup of tea.
And thinking of the Christmases that they once knew
That now were pushed aside as older they grew.
Yes, Christmas is for children and that is all well known.
But aren't we all children even when grown.
We have parents and our parents do too.
But, the best Parent of all is God who loves you.

Religious Poems

Did You Ever Wonder?

Did you ever wonder
about that child born so long ago
Predicted by others
that all on earth might know?
Did you ever wonder
why our great God in Heaven above
Wanted to take care of us
with His undying love?
Did you ever wonder
why He sent His only begotten Son,
To suffer and die on the cross
to help save everyone?
The answer is in the Bible
and we all know 'tis true
Jesus died upon the cross
because He loved me and you.
But at the cross is not
where this love story doth end.
For He arose from the grave
and walked on earth again
Then miraculously ascending
unto His heavenly throne.
Yet on earth for us,
His blood still does atone.

I Am

I am,
I am the Christ who died.
I am,
I am the one they crucified.
I am,
I am the resurrected one.
I am,
I am God's Holy Son.
Believe in me
And one day you
Will be in Heaven
With me, too!

Time For God

My time with God had slowly dwindled.
Passion for Him needed rekindled.
Unimportant things had taken hold.
My fire for God was growing cold.
My life was getting out of control.
I needed to reinforce my goal
So I let go of things that were not important
And I let go of things that were not relevant.
For God will help me find my way
When I make time for Him each day.

Jesus In My Heart

I don't know about you,
but I know about me.
I have Jesus in my heart
And now I'm sin free.
My heart was black
And heavy with sin,
But now it is white
And I have peace within.
I was living a life
That was full of shame.
Now I am proud of my actions
Thanks to His glorious name.
I can tell you from experience
That life can get you down,
You may wrestle with problems
And wear a permanent frown.
But, with Jesus in your heart
You can have a big smile
Because He'll walk with you,
Every step, every mile.

My Goal

My only goal is to reach Heaven's shore
Where earthly things will bother me no more.
I'll wander those streets paved with gold
And meet with prophets from days of old.
God will smile and take my hand
And lead me through this promised land.
Heaven's the place I want to be,
Praising God through all eternity.

God Is There With Me

From the mountains so high
To the valleys so low,
God is there with me
Helping me grow.

In a vast city
Or a lone country road
God is there with me
To carry the load.

Sometimes my heart's heavy
And burdened with care
But I know God is with me
He'll always be there.

God will be with me
No matter the place.
God will be with me
With His marvelous grace.

God, I am thankful
I have your within
That you took my life
And rid me of sin.

I Hear A Song

Sitting in church I hear a song
That keeps my heart singing all the day long.
I look at the people sitting in each pew
And wonder if they feel the same as I do,
About God's love and His wonderful grace
That keeps us going through life's hectic race.
I'm so thankful that he saved my soul
And to be with Him in glory is my constant goal.

Thinking of Jesus

I love to think of Jesus
I love to ponder on His name
And how He helped others
How He helped the lame.
I love to read about Him
In my Bible every day.
And after every reading
This is what I say"
"I love you Jesus,
I hold You in my heart,
And from your knowledge
I will never part."

I Love To Think Of Jesus

I love to think of Jesus.
I think of Him everyday.
I think of how He loves me.
And helps me find my way.
I want to be more like Him
And help others know Him too.
But first I must consider
All the things that I must do.
I must thoroughly read the Bible
And study every word I read.
Not just rely on what I've heard
But to know just what I need.
Sometimes I think of Him
When traveling down the road
He makes the day seem brighter
And lightens up my load.
I'll always think of Jesus
In good times and in bad.
He can brighten up the day
When I am feeling sad.

A Song In My Heart

I heard a song, 'twas a beautiful sound
It spoke about God and being heaven bound
And keeping your feet on the upward way
Following Jesus every hour of the day.
I listened closely to that beautiful tune
And the words I memorized so very soon.
Now I do walk with a song in my heart
Knowing that from Him I will never part.
As I go along singing, I visualize
How wonderful God is and so infinitely wise.

Have You Heard

Have you heard the story
of the Christ who died for you?
It is written in the Bible
and every word of it is true.
Have you heard the message
that He brought for you and me?
Have you read it in the Bible,
for it comes to you for free?
It was God's only Son
who died upon that tree.
Have you heard of the torture
and how His body they did maim
And it only made Him stronger
for Jehovah was His name.
Jehovah! Jehovah! Jehovah was His name.

Poem of Praise

Lord I praise and worship you
Please hear my humble prayer.
There are things I just don't understand
So I've placed them in your care.
Help me to become more like you
In all matters of my life.
Help me sort out the things
That add to my daily strife.
Thanks for listening to me Lord
As I kneel here and pray.
For I truly love you Lord Jesus
More and more each day.

Glorify the Lord

Glorify the Lord in all you do.
Letting others know His Word is true.
Tell them He's the only one they can turn to.
When they must build their lives anew.

Trust in Him with all your heart and mind.
You will find His love so sweet and kind.
There's no truer friend you'll find
Who is so faithful and refined.

You can take your heartaches to the Lord.
There's no better gift you can afford.
On this sacred journey jump aboard.
Then we'll all be in one accord.

This journey leads us to a Holy place
Where all God's children will embrace.
The trials of this earth He will erase
And in Heaven we'll see Him face to face.

Do I Show It?

Do my actions even show
What my words want you to know?
Does my attitude show I care
When my love for God I share?
Does my heart make you feel
That my love for God is real?
Have my words given you hope
So with problems you can cope?
The Bible explains it all
That on Jesus we must call.

I Need You

Oh, why am I weary, and why am I sad?
I long to be happy, I long to be glad.
Oh, my heart feels heavy with troubles and woe.
What can I do to get help? Where should I go?

I have lost the will to go on every day.
So I need to get down on my knees and pray
For God's ever lasting love to fill my life
And take away all my misery and strife.

God I love and trust you so very much.
Please come into my heart with your tender touch.
And erase the ugly black spots in my heart
And help me, Lord, to others your love to impart.

Follow Jesus

Just know that we face burdens and hardships in this life.
Everyone should know the Bible teaches how to lessen our strife.
Satan tries to tear us away form the true message of God's word.
Using deceit to frustrate and neutralize all that we have heard.
So clear your mind of Satan's mundane and deceitful guise.

And follow **Jesus**, for your reward awaits you in the sky.

Faith In The One

What does the future hold?
Sickness or wealth untold?
Jesus is in the One
Who is the only Son
Of the One up above
Who sent Him in Love
To save us from sin.
A new life to begin

Looking forward each day
To finding a new way
To live a good life
That may be full of rife
Because of His promise
I'm not a doubting Thomas
But live in the joy
His word to employ.

The Great Spirit

She whose hair shimmers with the light from the moon
Whose voice mimics the song of the bird
She whose hands know the earth and the wind,
In whose heart speaks the words of the storm
While breathing the breath of the butterfly.
She whose laughter echoes from the sky
And whose silence claps with thunder.
She whose arrow follows a straight path
But wavers at the forked trail.
She who can hurdle the highest mountain
Yet falter over a grain of sand.
She who meshes with my heart
Draws blood from my eyes
Fills my veins with frozen water
Warms my world with her being.
The Great Spirit gives her the gift
of gentleness to all creatures.
Her heart mourns with laughter
And celebrates with pain the inequities of justice.
She's like a child with wrinkled skin
And an ancient one who longs for the milk of its mother.
Burdened with the desires of the world
Yet restrained by knowledge and truth.
She searches each niche to try to fill it with her being
Her tears float upon the sea, yet do not taste of the salt.
There's a longing in her breast that sears deep
to the pit of her stomach and aches in her bowels.
The Great Spirit felt the heat of her agony many years ago.
He sent a gift to her--- a gift from His own flesh.

A gift that cools the fires
And guides her arrow to the right fork in the trail
A gift that removes the thunder from her silence,
The grain of sand from her path.
It makes the niche fit her being
Yet asks for nothing but acceptance.

Love the Lord

Love the Lord with all your heart.
That's how your day should always start.
Do not stray; just do your part
And from your side he will not depart.

Love the Lord with all your soul.
Make that your life's daily goal.
This way His name you will extol
And make your heart feel really whole.

Love the Lord with all your mind.
And at His table daily dine.
And if you're really so inclined
You will benefit all mankind.

Love the Lord with all you strength.
And follow His road to its full extent.
You'll find your faith has been renewed
And you will feel His love anew

("Love the Lord your God with all your heart
and with all your soul
and with all your strength
and with all your mind"
and "Love your neighbor as yourself"
Luke 10:27 NIV}

Dear Mr. Lucifer

The searing look from those heinous black eyes,
Constricts like a venomous snake.
The fear I have of you has developed over time
Creating in my heart this terrible ache.
Leave me alone, go away, you're like an alpha ray
You destroy everything that comes your way
You are despicable: you enhance my wrath.
Move aside; don't cross my path.
I wish to destroy every fiber of your being
Mr. Lucifer, I demand you be fleeing
I have a more purposeful life to live
The one my Heavenly Father has to give.
One without fear and trepidation
I owe Him all my acclamation.
The earth will be a safer place
When God our hearts truly embrace.

God Sent His Son

God sent His Son,
His only one
To carry the load
Down a lonely road
Knowing full well
He in Heaven would dwell.
From His throne above
He sends us His love.
His life He did share
So we could prepare
To live with Him forever
When earth's ties we sever.
On the cross He died
To save people worldwide.
But He rose again!
And we all say, "AMEN,"

Let Christ Dwell In You

After reading the Bible last night for a while
I went out for a walk and walked nearly a mile.
The evening skies were gray and the winds caused a chill.
As I pondered God's words and the truth of His Will.
Do I have enough strength, enough courage today,
To say, "Yes, yes, my Lord", I will follow your way.
Each step took me farther and farther from home
As I thought about going to Athens or Rome.
These were not the dreams that I had made for myself
Did God want me to hide these away on some shelf?
Being a school teacher was my only desire
But I did not want to see God's terrible ire
After all, His plan would be better than mine
And I would not, no would not, just sit there and whine.
So, I traced my steps home and went wearily in
Not to follow God's Will would absolutely be sin.
But the feeling wasn't quite in my heart
So I went to the Bible and the pages did part.
And I hoped that God would have a message for me.
That I could accept whatever it be.
As the message came and it came clear and strong
I merely had interpreted his first message wrong.

In Colossians 3:16 it says,
"Let the word of Christ dwell in you richly, teaching…..(NIV)

This Is The Day The Lord Has Made

Got up this morning and the sun didn't shine.
Looked at the clock, It was quarter to nine.
Said, "Lord, this day don't look so fine."
So I sat right down and started to whine.

Got up this morning, it was cloudy and gray.
Just don't like it when it looks this way.
I like best a bright sunny day
Cause then the kids can go out to play.

Got up this morning, the rain was pouring down.
And then looked down at my old ragged gown.
I sat in my chair and just started to frown.
As I listened to the baying of my old coonhound.

Got up this morning, it was thundering loud.
I looked outside at that old black cloud.
Then I sat down and my head I bowed
And thanked God for this day He'd allowed.

Got up this morning from the bed where I'd lain.
Wonderin' what's behind that window shade.
But, I knew that all my worries would fade
'Cause this was the day that the Lord had made.

"This is the day the Lord has made:
Rejoice and be glad in it".
(Psalms 118:24 NIV)

A Glorious Day

I've left behind my burdens and strife.
My heart feels happy with the joys of life.
I look at myself in the mirror and say.
It's going to be a most glorious day.
I believe this is true because you see,
I know Jesus loves me and He set me free.
So every day I'll sing His praise.
And, every day His banner I'll raise
And let all know that He is the King
Who protects us under his merciful wing.

Love Your Enemies

Love your enemy as yourself
Don't place them back
On some dusty shelf.
Pray for them with an open heart.
Forget the hurt they did impart.
It does no good to have bad feelings
When with your enemies you are dealing.
So you must pray for them right now
That they might change their hearts somehow.
This could let God enter and save their soul.
For this is God's plan; this is His goal.

Share The Word

One day I thought I heard God say,
"Do you think my Word you can obey?
I looked around; my head did bow.
I said, "God, I want to. Please show me how."
I did not know what to expect
But, His Will, I would respect.
I wondered if my life would change
Would He ask me to go someplace strange?
"Share My Word," is what He asked.
It is not a difficult task.
Read the Bible with open heart.
That's the very best way to start.
Then memorize and meditate
Then you can articulate.
People need the Word everywhere
To get out of the Devil's lair.
There are things people need to know,
Before they can spiritually grow."
"God," I said, in my shy, quiet voice,
"I do not speak publicly by choice."
Then God whispered in my ear
Ever so gently, so I could hear.
"If someone had not shared with you,
Would you the Christian life pursue?
Why not take your pen in hand?
And, that way take your Christian Stand?

Peace Within

Sometimes my life seemed such a jumble
Each step I took I seemed to stumble
But then I found another way
To see me thru each passing day.
I found Jesus and took Him in.
And now my life is free of sin.
I no longer grumble and groan
I no longer feel alone
I now have peace within my heart
Since Jesus plays a major part.

Cinquians

(Cinquains are challenging and fun to write.
Cinquains are 5 line poems with:

line 1 having 2 syllables;
line 2 having 4 syllables;
line 3 having 6 syllables;
line 4 having 8 syllables;
line 5 having 2 syllables.

He Lives

Christ lives!
He lives today
He died for you and me.
To save our souls and set us free
Amen

Joy

What Joy
He gave His Son
To save our souls from sin
To make our hearts feel clean again.
Rejoice!

Baby Jesus

The Child
Small and Holy
Born in a lowly manger bed
Wise Men came and gave precious gifts.
Jesus!

The Book

Bible
The Holy Book
Inspired by God Himself
Teaching the way of salvation
Read it!

The Promise

Rainbow
Promise from God
Arching across the sky
Reminder of His love for us.
Faithful.

The Blood

His Blood
He shed for me
To take away my sin
Shed upon that Calvary cross
Cleansing.

Love

God's Love
Gentle and Kind
Makes my heart swell with pride
To know that he loves me so much
Great Love.

Church

Building
A Holy place
So joyful and peaceful
Praises and songs worshiping Him
My Church

The Sinner

Sinner
Needs Christ inside
To help him see the light
To cleanse his heart and make it white
Needs help.

Praise

Dancing
Singing a song
Making a joyful sound
Bowing heads and saying a prayer
Praising.

God

God's here
In all the earth
Leading us forever more
Protecting us with His great Love.
So dear.

My Friend

Jesus
Knows me
Understands me
Loves me and cares for me always
My friend.

Other Poems

Looking Forward

The days I cherished as so dear
Those days of old no longer here.
The present now abounds in me
The past has duly set me free.
I look forward to everyday
To the joys the present does convey.
I look around at nature's art
'Cause it can fill and empty heart
I start each day with a little prayer
As God's wonders I declare.

A Better State of Mind

The sights and sounds of yesterday
are ringing through my head.
I hear them every day and night
even when I'm in bed.
The laughter, the tears, the smiles the cheers
bring back those days so dear.
I'd love to share them with my friends,
but they're no longer here.
Alas, I look around and see
that time is passing by.
The things I used to love to do
I think of with a sigh.
And then I take another look
at what is happening now.
I find that things are very good
and this I do avow.
Life has not passed me by,
it's been carrying me along.
I feel it in the summer winds
and in the Sparrow's song.
I can smell the sweet blossoms
of the honeysuckle tree.
My present life is wonderful
and this I do agree.
The past too was wonderful
and a pleasant place to live.
The present offers so much more
and has so much to give.
I will remember yesterdays

but leave them all behind.
For I've found that today
can bring a better state of mind.
Don't revel in the memories
of all those yesterdays.
Make memories of the present
and give them their due praise.

A Morning Walk

A morning walk through the fresh dew's glory
A perfect blend for an exciting story
An unplanned walk—destination unknown
A walk through the woods—just me alone
The birds heralding the morning light
Each on their own dutiful flight
The scant grasses wet beneath my feet
Queen Ann's Lace a beautiful treat
A timid brown hare dashes away
Spooked by my intrusion this day
Few enjoy this morning's splendor
That dawn doth so proudly render
As the sun creeps over the earth's crest
I watch in wonder and full of zest
But I delight in this time so neat
I find it a most glorious treat

Dreams

Locked in reality, unsure of ourselves
Our dreams are hidden away on mental shelves.
We doubt possibilities that lie ahead.
To venture o'er the horizon causes dread.
To pursue our dreams is far beyond our reach.
The future is an anticipated breach.
Fearing the real presence of reality,
We cower behind its actuality.
Afraid of trying each possibility
Forever we fear their viability.
We fail to venture into the land of dreams
Being farfetched and bordering the extremes.
Efforts and actions leading us into naught
Seeming failures causing us nothing but fraught.
Fearing taunts and criticism from others
Dreams being debased by those we call brothers.
But dreams are achievements we have not yet reached.
They conquer the future and should be beseeched.
The world sees dreams as abstractions from real life.
They view the dreamer as just one full of strife.
Not realizing how much they add to our life.
Progress in history means a dream was pursued.
This is how all dreamers' dreams should be viewed.
Failure can strengthen and reveal the dreams goal.
So, the dreamer's dream we should try to extol.
Dream with confidence and determination.
Keep following your dreams and aspirations
And keep on dreaming without hesitation.
Progress will happen with real dedication.

A True Friend

Hard to find is a friend like you;
Always patient and kind 'tis true.
Unquestioning joy, effusive,
A truer friend could never live.
Always near and trying to please.
With me you feel so much at ease.
You would never abandon me.
On this matter we do agree.
You never hold a grudge, just joy,
If undue tactics I employ.
Unkind words can make you cower
When I assert too much power.
You quiver with love, never wrath
When my anger crosses your path.
You always stay right by my side
Keeping in step with every stride.
For safety, on you I rely.
You keep an ever-watchful eye.
I will trust you implicitly
For you love me explicitly.
A true companion I have found
In this, my dog my faithful hound.

Snow

Colors of the day dimmed by a thick hazy sky:
Midday sun hidden from an ever-watching eye.
Our bodies move more from obligation than joy
As the cold bitter winds force warm clothes to employ.
We see a sliver of white sailing in the breeze.
Surely it is the first flake that comes down to tease.
Considered the leader…for many will follow.
Around us they fly, soon the world they will swallow.
They're like a family of flakes falling to the earth
Shaping the surroundings with new art forms of worth.
Strong winds whipping it around into different shapes
As through it we all try dutifully to traipse.
The former drabness of the day now disappears
As the beauty of each snowflake perseveres.
Since each drifting snowflake forms the power of snow,
Upon us all it's beauty and force doth bestow.

The Old Church

Proudly stood the old gray stone church,
Bell hanging from her lofty perch.
Built long ago with sweat and pride,
Once God's presence was felt inside,
Transforming many people's lives.
The aura of love still survives.

Worshipers of long ago mourn.
Her present state leaves them forlorn.
But, alas, she exists no more.
Gone the church they all did adore.
Their eyes still tearing at the sight.
Viewing the churches final plight.

Stolen is the brass from the doors.
Dusty cobwebs litter the floors.
Glass stained windows ripped from her walls.
Rain washes down the stately halls.
The bell's ringing no longer heard
As the vandals plunge undeterred.

Many lives were impacted here
Who held this edifice so dear.
Here many a man took a wife
Pledging to God a Holy life.
Newborns were taught how to survive
A Godly life would help them thrive.

Only an empty shell stands now.
No one enters, his head to bow
The church now shows such great decay
This elysian church of yesterday.
Is it an eyesore, nothing more?
Oh, no! It holds their dreams of yore.

Embracing the Future

Pioneers bravely crossing the sea,
Traveling far from where they used to be.
They went boldly to a strange new place
Different people and language all to embrace.
Fulfilling their dreams and their ambitions.
No turning back. Making transitions.

Each of us can become pioneers
With challenges. Overcoming fears.
New strange places, new destinations.
Reveling in new expectations.
Rewards, disappointments, there may be.
But onward we strive never to flee.

What lies ahead, we do not know.
But, onward we tread; onward we go,
Whatever's ahead may be revealed.
The journey as yet is still concealed.
Praying for strength and love on our way
Knowing that God is with us each day.

Travel the path not herded by time.
Treasures that await are all sublime.
Love's the answer, so love each other.
Good or evil each is a brother.
Stand firm in beliefs that you now face,
Anticipating that wondrous place.

Solace

Memories meandering through my mind
Thoughts of yesterday clearly defined.
Things for which I still do yearn
Longing for innocence to return.

Happier days from my youth I find
Within my soul so deeply confined.
Each breath inhaled brings inspiration
Each breath exhaled brings exultation.

Not committed to life's dreary tasks
Just doing daily what the soul asks.
Desires and goals now seem so distant.
Woes of my heart remain consistent.

In the sanctuary of my soul
I find no purpose; I find no goal.
God help me, I need some breathing space.
Help me find SOLACE in Your Great Grace

The Argument

He crossed the street, destination unknown.
Through the cold wet rain he walked all alone.
His hatless head soaked from the cold wet rain,
Hot tears were shed that he could not contain.
His heart was heavy as he trudged along.
Why had he argued he knew it was wrong.
He longed to go home and set things aright.
But that last scene left an unpleasant sight.
They'd quarreled about some trivial things
And now in his heart a hurtful song sings.
He loved her dearly. Now things were awry.
He longed to hold her and make her not cry.
The chilling cold rain running down his face
Confirmed his desire to find a warm place.
He wanted that place to be home 'twas true.
But those hurtful words were hard to subdue.
As he moved forward, a figure appeared
With long dark hair and a matching long beard.
He thought to run from this unknown feature
But kind, soothing words came for this creature.
'Twas a gentle voice that he could embrace.
And he envisioned a kind gentle face.
It urged him to return to his dear wife
And end this battle that had caused them strife.
He listened intently to what was said
And decided no more tears should be shed.
Retracing his steps to his humble abode
This heavy burden he now wished to unload.
As he opened the door, there his wife stood.

Smiling up at him as he hoped she would.
He explained to her the vision that came
He didn't know who it was or even his name.
She said to him in her soft gentle voice,
He came to me also with the same choice.
We had never seen him before this night,
But he helped us to make everything right.
We don't know how he came or how he went,
We only know he was heaven sent.

Merely Mortals

In this life there is no time to flit and dart
Among the fibers of our heart.
Emotions are readily torn asunder
Like the claps of pounding thunder.
When loved ones leave this earth for good
We may wonder for what they stood.
Was it for true righteousness,
Or merely just capriciousness?
On earth we are merely mortals
Waiting to pass through those eternal portals.

Different

(A perspective on bullying)

I'm different than you, not the same.
Not allowed to play in your game.
Why did you call me that awful name?
Is it because that I am lame?

I know I don't look exactly like you
But can't you accept somebody new?
I don't even speak like you "tis true.
And because of that my friends are few.

I feel like knives are stabbing my heart.
I would gladly step up and do my part.
I know I'm not dumb; I'm really smart.
I'd really like to have a fresh start.

At times I feel like I just want to die.
My brain is hurting. It wants to cry.
Can't you see I'm willing to try?
Can't you like me or give me a try?

Alone I walk down the busy street;
Walking slowly and shuffling my feet;
Wishing for just one friend to meet.
I guess I'll just have to stay discreet.

Poem about Writing a Poem

I tried to write a poem
as the teacher had asked.
I tried and tried to write one
but it seemed an awful task.
I have to choose a subject
to write about 'tis true
But what that subject ought to be,
I haven't a single clue.
Should I write something
that expresses strong emotion?
I just can't think of anything,
I've not a single notion.
Should it be a limerick
or a simple rhyming verse.
Perhaps it should be more blunt
and very, very terse.
I don't know! I've tried them all
and I just can't seem to think.
I guess I'll just have to settle down
and find some common link.
My head is full of empty thoughts
like balloons floating in the air.
I just can't seem to write
a single poem to take and share.
I really wanted to write it
just the way that I ought.

My efforts seem so useless.
I just seem to be so fraught.
Since this little tirade of mine
has been written down in rhyme
I'll just give it to the teacher
and hope she finds it sublime.

Another Halloween

Heaviness creeps over me as I look into the night.
Darkness crawling all around gives me a fright..
Eerie scratching noises seem to surround me
Burning nerves tell me I should quickly flee.
The ugly, musty smell of death is all around
I gather all my courage and away I bound.
Another Halloween has done its work
As all those creepy creatures sit and smirk!

Thoughts on Writing

Writing can mean a lot of things
Like writing a song for one who sings.
Or maybe the recognition it brings
When being published and soaring on wings.
It's a way of releasing an emotion that stings
The heart that a slanderous person slings.
But writing is tied to the heart with strings
As my mind digs deep into the heart, it clings
And develops a story or poem that rings
Into the heart of noblest kings
Writing is something that is never boring
Because it keeps both heart and mind soring.

Writing

Trying to write a few words
But nothing seems to come.
So I just sit here thinking
And feeling mighty glum.
Many thoughts run through my head
But soon they fade away.
I guess my brain is saying
Come back another day.
Another day has come and gone
But still no words I write.
It seems my brain has taken
Another winsome flight.
The paper is still empty
On the table where it sits.
And hopefully someday
I will find my writing wits.

My Writing Space

My writing space, where can it be?
In my head it's plain to see.
Electrical impulses and fibrous matter
All mixed up in silent clatter.
Thoughts whirling like a spinning top,
I don't think they will ever stop.
Things I see, hear, touch, smell and taste
Within my brain have all been placed,
Someday they'll burst out on written page.
Like an actor performing on the stage
They come dancing out of their hiding place
Lining up on the paper, choosing their space.
Does my brain feel empty? No, not a chance,
The impulses are still alive doing their dance.

Aspirations

As I run through this hectic race,
I see a void, an empty space.
I no longer rely on things acquired
But long for what my heart aspires.
I search for a simple distant place
Where all my thoughts I can embrace.
But all ambitions, hopes and fears
Are locked up in my burning tears.

Spring

Spring is in the air.
There's an aura of it everywhere
In refreshing cool showers
And colorful Spring flowers.
In the musky smell of the woods
Children romping in neighborhoods.
Even bees humming around their hive
These are the things that bring Spring alive.

Lonely Creature

Nobody loves me.
Nobody cares.
Nobody likes me.
Nobody dares.
The sight of me
Scares everyone.
I'm the loneliest creature
Under the sun.
On eight legs I crawl around.
When I come close,
I don't make a sound.
I hide under beds and other places.
I crawl on your walls and your shoelaces.
People scream when I come near.
They want to squish me out of fear.
So long cruel world, I say goodbye.
For your crushing boots made me die!

Nature Cycles

Rooted to the earth
Arms cold and bare
Shivering in the wind
He doesn't care.
The crown upon his head
Put to rest
on a leafy bed.
Enduring the elements
of nature
Without fear.
For he knows that winter
is already here.
He knows his Maker
He's no faker.
The oak tree nods its head at me
Because he knows nature cycles
And Spring will come again.

Human Revival

Life begins
Life ends
God gives us life
With the Love he sends.
Life has its ups
Life has its downs
It has laughs and tears
And it has its frowns.
We die a little every day
We try to hide it
With games we play
Ever seeking friends
And recognition
But losing out
Of our own volition.
Our thoughts forever
Becoming history
While our ambitions
Are still a mystery.
Gone are my friends
They're all behind
Sometimes I think
They were only in my mind.
The love I felt
Once upon a time
Was sweet and tender
And so sublime.
Now, lost forever
For eternity it seems
Living only in my heart

Or in my dreams
Caused by the
Elements of life
Hidden by remorse
In the sanctuary of strife.
But life has a way
Of reviving itself
Putting remorse away
On a remote shelf
Clawing up and out
Of the depths of our soul
Grasping at whatever
Gives us control.
The capacity to survive
An amazing feat
Avoiding hopelessness
That was once defeat
We become vibrantly excited
And full of hope
Viewing the world within our scope.
We view the past
And renew ourselves
Putting old habits
On distant shelves.
Determined to defy fate
Our dignity to retain
Aroused by the Spirit
Our soul is born again.
Revival having
Swept over us now
With this new hope
Our souls we endow.
We reassemble
The fragments of our lives
And from beginning to end
Humanity survives!

Dad's Roses

I picked a rose today
From the garden by the shed.
It had the sweetest smell
And was colored ruby red.
I placed it in some water
In a clear drinking glass
And placed it in the window
So all could see who passed.
It was planted by my father,
Who passed away last year.
Each time I see the roses
I wish that he were here.
I truly miss him dearly
From the bottom of my heart.
I wish that he could be here
His wisdom to impart.
His passion was for plants
And everything that grew.
He shared with everyone
Everything he knew.
His wisdom came to him
The old fashion way
By working in his gardens
Day after day after day.

(My Dad could make just about anything grow.
He was never lacking for beautiful flowers growing around his house.)

I Love You Mom

I cried as I sat beside her empty bed.
How many things had been left unsaid.
The silent voice inside my head
Uttering words that I hoped had been said.
My heart was weeping as I held her wedding band
Knowing for 74 years it had been on her hand.
She had been an adoring faithful wife
No matter the circumstances; no matter the strife.
Dad had already made his trip to the celestial shore,
And stood lovingly waiting for her at Heaven's door.
Sometimes things in life seem to obstruct our way
And there are so many things we don't take time to say,
Things like Thank You, I Love You, and I appreciated you, too.
But, most of all Mom, I hope you know, I truly did love you.
And now only precious memories –oh so dear.
Are what I have to cherish that keep you near.

Miss You

I sometimes feel lonely and blue.
It's hard the days to live through.
Always my heart thinks of you.
And all the things we use to do.

My lover you were from the start.
I thought that we would never part.
You were ingrained within my heart
When Cupid shot that tiny dart.

I know I'll miss you forever dear.
That's my minds greatest fear.
For death my broken heart did sear
When no longer you were here.

God Bless You

The months will come.
The months will go.
Warmed by the sun,
Chilled by the snow.
Each days challenges
Will seem so small
If upon God's mercies
You will call.
To so many others
You have been a friend.
Now to you
Their love they send.
Helping you in so many ways.
Live through these uncertain days.
So stay the same warm lovely you
And God will bless the things you do.

(This poem was written to a friend who had just lost her husband)

Modern Grandma and Grandpa

Grandpa hasn't changed a bit,
Except for the recliner in which he sits.
Grandma thinks she is so cool
The flip phone now her favorite tool.
Grandpa traded in his pitchfork too
Now he plays golf every day or two.
Grandma hides behind her shades
As she checks on her college grades
Upon the roof sits a satellite dish
For more TV is what they wish.
No more barns, no more hay
Just out gallivanting everyday.
No more chickens not a single cow,
Wouldn't have time anyhow.
Life has changed as you can see
And we're as happy as we can be.
The future may bring lots more stuff,
But for now we've got more than enough.
Perhaps!

(Just think how this poem changes our view
of the American Gothic painting)

The Unsinkable Ship

She bought a ticket for the maiden trip
On that most unsinkable ship.
Lavishly adorned everywhere
Even to the comfortable sundeck chairs.
The dining hall decorated with twinkling lights
Embellishing all the beautiful sights.
Ladies dressed in their most lavish attire
Strutting around till time to retire.
Men smoking their fancy cigars
Telling jokes and stories at the bars.
So many people boarded this boat
Twas a wonder it even stayed afloat.
The captain vouched for it's safe arrival
And all aboard were assured survival.
But as she peered out into the night sky
She felt a thud and let out a cry.
The ship had hit an iceberg just then
And she knew things were not as they had been.
Chaos soon grew to enormous heights
And then some passengers broke out in fights.
The ship eventually began its descent.
As the crowds continued their constant dissent
She went to her room and dressed in blue
For tonight she would die, she knew it was true.

(The RMS Titanic was a British passenger ship that sank in the North
Atlantic Ocean on April 15th, 1912 while on its way to New York City.)

My Husband's Yellow Plane

My husband built an airplane
It's such a pretty thing.
He painted it all yellow
With a brown stripe down the wing.

He puts on his pilot goggles
And sits in the pilot's seat;
Then revs up the engine
That doesn't miss a beat.

It roars and quivers and races
And then soars into the sky.
I sometimes sit and wonder
About this amazing guy.

Who takes bits and pieces
To build a flying machine
That's as beautiful as any
That I have ever seen.

He flies it in the morning
He even flies at noon
But never ever does he fly it
With the evening moon.

I would like to fly with him
But I know that I must not,
Because with extra weight
The engine gets too hot.

It's just a tiny plane
With a twenty foot wingspan
And only meant to hold
One solitary man.

So I will sit and watch
As through the sky he soars
Over the hills and lakes
And also the marshy moors.

And hope that from the vantage point
Where I am always standing
I will see him return and
Make his safe tail-dragger landing.

(My husband flew a hot air balloon, and an ultra-light before building
his own airplane. The only flying lessons he had were for the hot
air balloon. The license for the hot air balloon was acceptable for
flying the plane. So basically he taught himself to fly the plane.)

Back to Life

When he brought home that pile of junk
I sat down and my heart just sunk.
"A motor scooter", he had said.
I pictured something shiny and red.
"Well, what do you think," He said with a smile.
I answered him, but it took me a while.
"You said it was a fifty eight.
That's really something, that's really great.
It's a really nice crusty brown.
It could be fun to ride around town."
I didn't want to burst his bubble
So I said, "Maybe we could ride double."
He drug it through the big garage door
And started laying pieces all over the floor.
I heard a clink and I heard a clank,
And I'll tell you--and I'll be frank
I didn't think he could bring that scooter to life.
I should know since I'm his wife.
I went out later to look at the mess,
And to my surprise, he was making progress.
I asked if I could lend a hand.
He said, "Lay these bolts by that bent kickstand."
I could see in his face the look of joy
That a little child has with a brand new toy.
He used lots of tools, mostly wrenches.
And started laying parts along the benches.
Some to discard, some to keep.
Some to replace if he finds them cheap.
Sand it, paint it, polish it shiny

Fix the seat so it fits his hiny.
Now the paint looks so bright and red,
And with his helmet upon his head
He starts it up and takes his first ride
While I stand back and watch with pride.
And I can tell you now, since I'm his wife,
He brought that Cushman back to life.

(We were members of the Cushman Club of America and
eventually he restored 3 more Cushman scooters)

Life

I've got four kids and a house to clean,
A phone that rings and no time between.
A self-employed husband; I do the bookwork.
Oh! I wish I had some coffee, but the pot won't perk.
The floor is dirty and needs to be scrubbed.
But one of the kids say, "I need to be loved".
So, I sit and rock and give her a hug,
And wish that the vacuum would sweep the rug.
The clock strikes ten, I think about lunch.
But, the kids had no breakfast, so I guess I'll make brunch.
The cat had kittens and wants to be fed.
I give her some milk and a little bread.
The last litter's still hanging on the back screen door.
Now what will I do with another four more?
The clothes hamper is full and about to burst,
And I just can't decide which load to do first.
The washing machine just hardly works
The tub won't spin till I give it a jerk.
The agitator won't jump without a bump.
If the clothes didn't get clean I'd throw it in the dump.
The skies are gray the wind is chill
I check the mail and here come the bills.
Oh no! A refund on an overpaid bill;
Things are looking up, what a thrill.
The phone rings, a customer calls,
As I try to take a message the youngest one bawls.
I sit on the couch and the stuffing falls out.
I look at the ragged chairs and I just want to pout.
And then I remember what life's all about.

Complainin' won't help but prayin' will.
It makes those troubles just seem so nil.
My Bible is near and I pick it up.
I know I need Jesus, not just good luck.
So I thanked God then and there,
That I'm where I'm at instead of who knows where.

It Hurts

She dried her tears and went to bed.
It hurt, the things the others said.
They made fun of how she dressed
Even though it was her best.
She pulled the blankets way up high
And then let out a mournful sigh.
Lord, please let the others see
That I am content just being me.
I don't need fancy clothes to wear
Or baubles dangling in my hair.
For I have something in my heart
Of which you are the greatest part.
I would really just like someone to say,
"Please, won't you come with me and play".

The Carnival Dress

The dress was pink and it fit me fine.
I got it for my birthday when I was nine.
Mother made it from a flower sack
She could sew nicely, she had the knack.
It had flowers and was a light pale pink.
The most beautiful dress I'd ever had, I think.
A carnival happened to be in town that day.
We walked to it 'cause 'twas only four blocks away.
As we approached we heard the music of a Merry-Go-Round.
That was the very first place we were bound.
Then cotton candy and elephant ears.
And the fortune teller with her shiny glass sphere.
The fun house gave us quite a scare,
But we went through again on a double dare
The Ferris wheel was so much fun
But then all of a sudden the rain begun.
We hurried home as the rain poured down.
As did everybody else in that town.
My dress was as soaked as it could be
And now no longer did it fit me.
Mother helped me strip off the dress
With laughter she could not suppress.
The dress had shrunk in the pouring rain.
And would never, ever fit me again.
From a potato sack the dress was made.
It should have been shrunk first I'm afraid
Mother said with a mournful frown.
I'm afraid I have let you down.
Please, Mother, do not feel sad.
It is still the prettiest dress that I ever had.

I Feel Patriotic

I feel patriotic when the US flag passes by
Displaying its stripes against a clear blue sky.
I stand erect; on my heart place my hand
Revering the flag makes me feel so grand.
I love the colors—red, white and blue.
Each time I see them my heart skips anew.
The stars on its corner like the stars in the sky
Symbolizes to me that it will always fly high.

I feel patriotic when the national anthem is played
By the band marching in a Fourth of July parade.
I sing all the words as the band plays on
It resonates in my head even when the band is gone
As I listen I raise my head and close my eyes
And just like Francis Scott Key, I can see the Flag waving high.
Yes, I can stand with pride with the rest of the throng
As they play the Star Spangled Banner, my countries song.

I feel patriotic with the Bible in my hand,
Because we have freedom of worship in this great land.
Yes, freedom of worship and freedom of speech
And freedom to exceed as far as we want to reach.
And if I don't agree with all the things that you do
Getting along with each other can always ensue.
I admire this country for what it has done for me
For it lets me be whatever I want to be.

Love Poems

What Is Love?

Love is a whirlwind of emotion.
A time of exasperating devotion.
A time you feel deep in your heart
The two of you will never part.
Love will in your heart entwine
And wrap itself around your mind.
A time you want to run and shout
And let your feelings all come out.
You want to say, I love you dear
And keep that person always near.

How You Make Me Feel

As I think of you
My heart cannot conceal
The awesome wonder
Of how you make me feel
I have loved you
From the very start
And my heart tells me
That we will never part.
I know we love each other
In a very special way
And I will always cherish you
Until my dying day

Love Intensified

Love has no meaning
without you by my side
And each day with you
my love's intensified.
As every day goes by,
I love you more and more.
For I know you are the one
I really do adore.
So I'll keep you in my heart
forever and a day.
For you're the one I'll love
now and alway.

Show Love to Each Other

There are many ways
to show love to each other.
Whether it be a friend
or even your brother.
Just give them a smile
with a twinkle in your eye.
And simply wave at them
when you are passing by.
It fills their heart with joy
and you feel better too.
By showing love to others
as you know that you should do.

My Love For You Can Only Grow

My love for you can only grow.
It seems as if that's all I know.
I could send you flowers and candy too,
But would that prove my love is true?
The thing I really want to show
Is how our love can really grow.
So I will hold your hand and say
I love you more each and every day.

Love Is

Love is like the morning light
Filling my heart from morn till night
Love is like a lulling breeze
Touching my heart with gentle ease
Love is like a lilting wave
Telling my heart it's something to save
Love is like a summer shower
Telling me I love you more each hour.
Love is like the sun above
Telling me you are the one I love
Love is having you by my side
And having God always as our guide.

The Man I Love

The man I love is by my side.
Our life has been a wonderful ride.
I love him dearly with all my heart.
That's where Cupid threw his dart.
We sometimes argue and have a spat.
But, we love each other in spite of that

I Love My Wife

I love my wife; she's as sweet as a dove.
That's why we met and fell in love.
She was the one God sent to me.
That is the way it was meant to be.
So we are living life day by day,
Me by her side all the way.